Minimalism

A Pragmatic Manual For Streamlining Your Living Space And Personal Life, Managing Your Finances To Promote Happiness, Well-Being, And Balance Using Established Minimalist Principles Tailored For Families

AndoniBastida

TABLE OF CONTENT

The Hazards of Excessive Clutter 1

It's Time To Organize Your Life: Make Space For Your Soul And Mind 12

The Meeting Point of Nomadism and Minimalism . 34

Minimalism's Advantages 64

The Essentialist 90

An overview of consumerism and minimalism 107

The answer? Less is more. 127

The Hazards of Excessive Clutter

Is it accurate that leading a minimalistic lifestyle can greatly enhance its quality? In actuality, they are but a handful of the advantages. In the long term, simplifying your life may be incredibly fulfilling.

You can have gathered items from presents, overseas trips, vacations, etc. It's also possible you've accumulated emotional stuff or held onto expensive items you wouldn't part with. Whatever your motivations, it's critical to realize that you must declutter your life and home.

The Brain's Effects of Clutter

If you're like most people, you might believe that retaining items—even ones you don't use or need—is generally innocuous. However, this isn't always the case because it can negatively impact your brain. It may also impact those in your immediate vicinity and other aspects of your life.

The constant gathering of items can develop into hoarding, a severe symptom of obsessive-compulsive disorder (OCD). A mental health condition known as anxiety and sadness, which can be crippling and keep you from participating in society regularly, can also be brought on by or made worse by an excessive connection to objects.

According to a Princeton University study, physical clutter reduces mental function, increases stress, and competes for attention. Excessive clutter around you impairs your ability to think clearly, focus on activities, and process information. A disorganized setting will cause you to become distracted. Similar research conducted at UCLA revealed that clutter inhibits creativity. When individuals handled their possessions, the researchers found that their levels of stress chemicals increased. The participants' cognitive processes were severely hampered by multitasking and organizing the clutter because their brains were overloaded.

Clutter just makes things more stressful and takes up precious time. Clutter lovers frequently experience irritation and worry. They struggle to unwind and frequently feel out of control. You should start a home and learn how to declutter to feel more at ease and be more productive.

Not Just Physical Clutter

Have you ever given your smartphone or computer a thorough inspection? How many alerts do you receive daily, and are they anything you want? It's possible that you haven't given digital clutter much thought previously. Your mind pauses whatever it's doing and concentrates on the notice every time you get one. Many individuals use their phones as their first tool in the morning and as their last thing to glance at before turning in for the night. Eliminating superfluous apps and notifications is crucial. Generally speaking, it's best to delete notifications that don't originate from real people. Probably the most clutter you can hold in one hand is your smartphone.

Because there is virtually no limit to the amount of digital clutter one can accumulate, it is crucial to regularly review one's files and remove any that are no longer needed. Applications and software that you no longer use should be uninstalled.

You might have obligations and clutter in your life. Have you ever felt that your mind is constantly occupied by hundreds of little tasks that need to be completed? Review your to-do lists and cross out any items that are not essential. In this manner, you can maximize your free time and concentrate on the things that matter. The things that will assist you in beginning to transform your life into what you desire should be at the top of your priority list. Fixing small issues can take an eternity, but addressing larger issues should come first.

In light of this, you ought to study effective decluttering techniques. Simply throwing things out won't cut it. The right methods for decluttering are the subject of the following chapter.

Section 1: Is a Minimalist Lifestyle Suitable for You?

To choose minimalism means to acquire only necessities. Minimalism is becoming a movement that will last longer than a fleeting fad, as living a life free of needless belongings is frequently much richer and fuller. Some people become a little uneasy when they hear "minimalist." For some individuals, the phrase may evoke images of blank walls, empty pantries, and poverty. However, minimalism is a personal choice that is often unrelated to scarcity.

Questions to Help You Decide If Minimalism Is Right for You

to determine whether you would succeed on this road. Consider the following inquiries for yourself:

Is Your Cleaning Too Excessive? Minimalism can be a blessing for people who feel like they are constantly working nonstop to keep their homes in functioning order. Reducing your possessions can lessen this requirement.

● Do You Feel Worried? Minimalism can assist in making your environment a better location for rest if you're one of the many Americans who suffer from excessive stress.

● Do You Owe Money? Reducing your possessions can help you make fewer payments on the things you need to pay for.

- Would You Like Extra Time? You may be surprised to learn how much time possessions consume—from shopping for them to keeping, arranging, and cleaning them. You may reclaim part of your time for yourself and the things you love by getting rid of them.
- Are You Concerned About the Climate? Because minimalism uses fewer resources and produces less waste, it helps lessen our environmental impact.
- Are You Pleased to Save Money? Spending less is not a requirement of minimalism, but it does present an excellent opportunity to do so. You may make better decisions and acquire long-

lasting, high-quality stuff when you buy fewer things.

● Do You Have No Fear Changing? By living a minimalistic lifestyle, you may prioritize your inner wants and self over fads and whims. This calls for some adjustments.

● Is Life Comprising More Than Material Goods? Minimalism is ideal for people who don't wish to find meaning in material stuff. Having too many possessions can easily lead to victimization, even for those who don't deliberately look outside themselves for significance.

You are special and precious because of your passions, spirit, and heart. Don't compromise your identity or your personal goals in an attempt to blend in with the masses. Too short a life for that. Your experience with simplicity will differ from others' experiences. Find the best method if this chapter struck a chord with you. You'll begin purging things from your life that you no longer need to create more time for the most important things.

It's Time To Organize Your Life: Make Space For Your Soul And Mind

* Begin organizing

Have you been overly preoccupied? Despite your best efforts, does the day seem to never end when you have a lot on your plate? It appears that you have amassed a significant amount of both material and immaterial trash. To avoid any kind of clutter, you must figure out how to simplify your life. So, how can you clear your mind and soul of all the clutter and reclaim your life? Start by living by the straightforward maxim, "Identify the important things in your life and purge the rest." Now, let's get going.

* Establish priorities

To help you understand what you want and don't want, make a list of priorities. Learning to prioritize is a key component of simplifying your life.

* Honor agreements

Making a list of your top priorities will assist you in fulfilling all of your obligations. Once you learn how to honor your promises, you will rarely experience excessive pressure for not meeting expectations.

* Be mindful of your time.

You should be aware of the value of your time. Consider your day's activities and how you utilize them. Redesigning and redefining your daily schedule is the aim. You will experience less stress the more you concentrate on being where you should be and doing what you should be doing.

* Make your work life simpler.

Our working lives are designed to be busy, so our schedules will never truly empty. There would always be work to be done till late at night and frustrating deadlines. Finish your most important tasks first to avoid feeling overburdened and mentally cluttered. Then, observe how everything else will fall into place flawlessly. Try applying the Pareto principle, or the 80/20 rule, to your work by dedicating 80% of your time to tasks that contribute 20% value and 20% of your time to tasks that offer greater value (20% value).

* Gently say "no."

Saying no is a very crucial skill to have. Being able to say "no" will make many things for you instantly simpler and spare you from needless effort. Additionally, it ensures that, even when you are convinced that you must fit this into your already packed schedule, you are not mentally burdened by things you must do for other people. Saying no will keep you trapped in pointless pursuits and activities.

* Limit pointless conversations

Eliminating pointless communication will make your life more tranquil, productive, and serene. Getting stuck in the many communication channels available to you is quite simple, such as emails, cell phones, instant messaging, Skype, online forums, Twitter, Facebook, and so on. You will most likely get disconnected from yourself if you spend too much time "connecting" with people. You may be confident that you will significantly lessen mental congestion and eventually achieve inner calm by reducing your time texting and using the internet.

* Make mental cleansings

Increase the time you spend engaging in activities aiding brain clearing and relaxation. Living a stress-free life can be greatly enhanced by establishing a regular meditation practice.

* Impulsive curbside shopping

Avoid becoming entangled in the materialism trap. You will run out of money quickly if you always intend to buy stuff after viewing their advertisements. Because advertisements frequently aim to arouse your desire for materialism, you may purchase an excessive number of pointless goods. A minimalist lifestyle will significantly lessen your never-ending need to acquire items that you don't even need, all of which have an impact on your mental clutter either directly or indirectly. You should watch less TV to see fewer advertisements, as this would prevent you from thinking about buying things just because you always see them on TV.

Follow your heart and mind

You can experience a sense of being trapped by so many desires that you find it difficult to find time for yourself. Spend some time doing things that bring you calm and tranquility. Take time to yourself to do the things you enjoy, whether it be dancing, singing, drawing, or relaxing. Don't neglect who you are. You would benefit from spending some time alone yourself. When your mind is completely at ease, full, and peaceful, you can give your all to your loved ones. See what happens when you try your hand at something you enjoy.

* Proceed steadily and slowly.

Here, "going slow and steady" means giving oneself enough time to complete some of the chores we sometimes take for granted or perform automatically. Take slow walks in the garden, drive slowly, drink coffee slowly, and eat your food slowly, among other examples. Because it teaches you to be present in the moment rather than doing things while your mind isn't even there, it will maintain you in good physical and mental health.

* Be present at the moment

Acquire the skill of living in the present and appreciating the current situation. It will not change if you think about the past, and it will not change if you imagine the future. Thus, keep your sanity by appreciating the day, moment, and circumstance you are in.

* Adopt a thrifty lifestyle

Living frugally does not mean decreasing expenses regularly. It alludes to the idea of wanting little and believing that we should leave fewer imprints on Mother Earth. To put it another way, simplicity is the key to inexpensive life. Determine your definition of "enough" and set a distinct boundary there. Demands that never stop would keep you caught in the consumerism cycle.

*Trash before purchasing

You must first choose what you can throw away before purchasing new stuff. Make the most of what you currently have by simplifying your environment, thoughts, way of life, and beliefs rather than hoarding more and more. As a result, you won't have to worry as much about where to keep them, when to use them, and how to maintain them. Consequently, you will have less mental congestion.

Section 4. Getting Rid of the Clutter

In the modern world, it's simple for clutter in our houses to accumulate over time. We keep acquiring new things while holding onto our old ones, and before we realize it, our possessions have buried us behind a mound of stuff.

Clutter consumes mental energy in addition to physical space. It may increase our stress levels and impair our ability to concentrate.

One of the first steps to minimalism and simple living is eliminating the clutter. Although it can be difficult, the correct attitude and method can make it a freeing and therapeutic experience. The following advice can help you declutter your home:

1. It can be difficult to declutter your entire house, so start with one room at a time. Rather, concentrate on one room at a time. Start with the area that irritates you the most, whether it's the kitchen, living room, or bedroom.

2. As you browse through every object in the room, divide it into three piles: Trash, Donate/Sell, and Keep. It is best

to maintain sentimental or valuable things you utilize regularly. Things that are in decent shape but are no longer useful to you should go in the Donate/Sell pile. Donated goods that are broken or unusable go into the trash pile.

3. Release your emotional attachments: We frequently cling to objects because of our strong feelings for them. Understanding that sentimental value and recollections are not correlated with material possessions is critical. When an object no longer uses you, give it some thought, cherish the memories it brings back, and then let it go.

4. Be brutal: We often convince ourselves that we should hold onto things we don't need. Ask yourself, honestly, if the thing makes you happy or adds value to your life. It's time to let it go if not.

5. Think about the 80/20 rule, which says that we only utilize 20% of our belongings 80% of the time. As you're going through your belongings, have this in mind. Are you clinging to items you seldom use or could live without?

6. Develop appreciation: While organizing your belongings, stop and express your gratitude for what you already have. Negative feelings resulting from parting with possessions can be lessened by concentrating on the good things in life.

7. Don't rush the process: It's crucial to remember that decluttering takes time. When necessary, take breaks, and don't feel pressured to complete everything in a single day. It is best to do it correctly and slowly.

We may create a serene, tranquil, and supportive space of a simpler way of life by decluttering our physical homes.

Recall that you just need to get rid of the items that are no longer necessary in your life. You don't need to get rid of everything.

Section Two

The Positive Effects of Minimalism on Mental and Physical Health

Decluttering and downsizing your belongings is only one aspect of minimalism; it also significantly affects our emotional and physical health. Embracing simplicity in our day-to-day activities has several advantages. This chapter will examine how minimalism might enhance our mental and physical well-being.

1) Enhanced Concentration and Efficiency:

Increasing attention and productivity is one advantage of adopting minimalism into our daily lives. By removing unnecessary items from our surroundings and minimizing distractions, minimalism can help us create a more ordered and effective setting. This can be accomplished by decluttering our homes and workplaces, cutting back on extra items, and streamlining our daily schedules. We may free up our minds and concentrate on the things that matter by simplifying our physical surroundings.

Eliminating pointless activities and distractions is another way minimalism can help us manage our time better. Our everyday activities can be made simpler to give us more time to concentrate on the things that are important to us and genuinely important. We may accomplish this by prioritizing our work, establishing clear objectives, and making a plan that fits our needs.

Additionally, minimalism can assist us in making better judgments about how we spend our time and become more aware of the things that matter. We can concentrate on the work rather than becoming sidetracked by unimportant information if we are alert and involved in the present moment. This may result in more output and a stronger sense of achievement.

2) Enhanced Emotional and Mental Health:

Better mental and emotional health is another advantage of adopting simplicity in our daily lives. By streamlining our lives and eliminating distractions and clutter, minimalism might help us feel less stressed and anxious. Clearing out unnecessary items may make our physical surroundings less distracting and more orderly. As a result, there may be a decrease in tension and anxiety and an increase in calm and happiness.

Furthermore, minimalism might enhance our emotional health by lowering the emotional burden that comes with material belongings. We can lessen feelings of guilt, shame, and connection to worldly possessions by parting with things that no longer fulfill us or make us happy. A stronger sense of independence and release may result from this.

Furthermore, minimalism might enhance our mental health by lessening the need to conform to consumer culture and cultural norms.

3) Improved Interactions:

By streamlining our daily schedules and providing more time and energy for the things that count, like spending time with friends and family, minimalism may enhance our relationships. We may reduce distractions and provide a more orderly and tranquil environment that enables us to be more present and involved in our relationships.

Moreover, minimalism can strengthen our bonds with one another by easing the tension and worry brought on by the need to conform to consumer culture and societal standards. Adopting a minimalist lifestyle allows us to focus on the things that matter to us and let go of the expectations from society to acquire material belongings. Our connections may become more genuine and connected as a result of this.

We can make space in our lives for the individuals most important to us because of this focus.

4) Enhanced Originality:

Our minds can be freed up, and more creative thinking and inspiration can flow when our surroundings are decluttered. Our minds become cluttered in an untidy environment, making it hard to concentrate on the task. By organizing our physical surroundings, we may free up our minds and make room for fresh concepts and opportunities.

Simplifying our everyday activities can boost creativity and clear out our physical area. We can devote more time and energy to creative endeavors by eliminating distractions and spending less time on repetitive work. Examples of this are writing, painting, and even coming up with concepts for new businesses.

Additionally, minimalism might encourage us to surround ourselves with things that inspire us and become more aware of them, which can foster greater creativity. We may foster an atmosphere that inspires and fosters creative thought by concentrating on what makes our lives meaningful and joyful.

5) Economical Savings:

Over time, minimalism can help us save money by lowering the amount we spend on pointless purchases. We can accomplish this by simplifying our lifestyle and clearing some belongings. We may clear up clutter, save money on storage costs, and make more room in our homes by eliminating things we no longer use or need.

Furthermore, minimalism might assist us in becoming more aware of our spending patterns and making wiser financial judgments. We may reduce our impulsive purchases and wasteful spending by concentrating on the things that matter and add significance to our lives. We may wind up spending less overall and saving more money.

Furthermore, minimalism might ultimately result in financial savings by lowering the need for costly maintenance and replacements. We may prolong the life of our belongings and lessen the need to replace them by treating them with care and using them sensibly.

6) Feeling in Charge:

Rather than feeling overtaken by clutter and diversions, minimalism can help us regain control over our belongings and lives.

Furthermore, minimalism can help us take charge of our finances by cutting back on wasteful spending and simplifying our way of living. We may take charge of our finances and make better financial decisions by making a budget, establishing clear financial goals, and paying attention to our spending patterns.

By streamlining our daily schedules and eliminating pointless chores and distractions, minimalism can also help us take charge of our time. We can take charge of our time and maximize it by prioritizing our chores and setting clear goals.

7) Enhanced Well-being:

By clearing out unnecessary items and distractions from our surroundings, minimalism can enhance our physical well-being by promoting better sleep, more energy, and sharper focus.

Chaos and stress brought on by clutter can harm our ability to sleep, feel energized, and generally be well. By decluttering and minimizing distractions, we may establish a more tranquil and well-organized setting that enhances our ability to unwind and sleep.

Additionally, by putting less time and effort into arranging and maintaining our belongings, minimalism might also help us feel more energized. By streamlining our everyday schedules, we can improve physical health by devoting more time and energy to physical activity.

These are only a handful of the numerous advantages minimalism offers us daily. Among the instances could be:

Enhanced Awareness of Oneself:

Increased feeling of emancipation and freedom

A more environmentally friendly way of living

And a ton more...

In summary, minimalism has a significant effect on both our mental and physical health. This chapter offers information on the mental and physical health advantages of minimalism, including how it can support rest and lessen stress, anxiety, and depression.

In the upcoming chapter, you will discover some helpful hints and efficient methods for decluttering your belongings.

The Meeting Point of Nomadism and Minimalism

Both in physical and digital settings less is more.

"Less is more" is a wise maxim that has endured and may be applied to digital and physical spaces. The famous quote "Less is more," credited to architect Ludwig Mies van der Rohe, captures a deep philosophical principle. It implies that clarity and simplicity are preferable to complexity and clutter in terms of design and deep understanding. This idea goes beyond simple beauty. One might uncover the essential beauty and truth of a thing, a concept, or life by eliminating the unnecessary. It promotes minimalism as a focused refinement where everything has a purpose, and nothing is unnecessary rather than as a lack. Less becomes more numerically and qualitatively richer in this sense, providing a deeper, more profound experience.

I've learned the value of minimalism from my travels, not only for my backpack but for my entire life. Allow me to explain how this applies to digital and real-world environments. Clutter reduction in your physical space is essential. A simple setting improves productivity and focuses attention. Imagine how liberating it would be to work in a tidy, open environment. Less stuff also translates into less time spent organizing and cleaning. And as time passes, I continue to discover new ways to make my life easier. This simplicity greatly lowers stress by fostering a sense of clarity and tranquility. Choosing sturdy, significant goods is better than amassing stuff; quality over quantity is important. It's also a success economically. Less shopping is better for the environment and saves more money. Let's talk about digital now. It's important to keep your digital area organized. Your office is on your laptop. You are slower with a cluttered phone or PC. Efficiency is increased through file and app cleanup, but the fight against spam and distractions never ends. Digital health is an additional factor. It might be stressful to get too many emails and messages. To keep my mind at ease, I filter my internet connections frequently. Safety is also a factor; fewer accounts equate to fewer cyberattack opportunities. Reducing your online presence is smart because phishing scams are becoming increasingly complex. Reducing the amount of data you have makes managing it easier. Having a simplified digital space makes backups easier and helps reduce loss. A clean digital workspace also promotes mental clarity, just like a tidy room.

Finally, exercise caution when using digital media. Join newsletters and channels that will improve your life. Every article should have a function or be enjoyable. Recall that less is frequently more in both the physical and digital spheres, particularly while moving constantly. We make certain that every item, application, and piece of material brings true value to our lives by deliberately selecting what takes up our time and space. By clearing the clutter from our external surroundings and making space for mental and emotional health, this method enables us to concentrate on the things that count.

Financial independence to support travel and exploration through simplicity.

Minimalism entails cutting costs and making the most of unnecessary assets to finance travel. I've mastered the art of minimalist living as a lifelong traveler to make the most of my adventures. Here's how to accomplish it as well. Reduce how many things you own to start. Garage sales and internet platforms are excellent venues to sell items you no longer need. If you own a property, consider leasing it. Short-term rentals are a great fit for websites like Airbnb. Reduce your regular outgoing costs. Resign from memberships you don't use, such as publications, streaming services, and possibly even your gym membership.

Additionally, consider less expensive internet and phone plans. Review your current residence. If you're not always on the go, downsizing can save money. To reduce expenses, think about living in shared housing. And is that car really necessary if you're constantly on the go? Walking, biking, and public transportation are more affordable and healthful options. Having a car may be very expensive, especially given the state of the economy. Owning a car comes with expenses that go well beyond the original cost of purchasing. One big monthly expense is car payments, particularly if the car is new or expensive. And then there's insurance, which always raises the monthly cost and varies based on several criteria like location, driving record, and automobile type. There is also the inevitable cost of maintenance. Although it can get expensive over time, regular maintenance is necessary for the vehicle's longevity and includes tire rotations, brake pad replacements, and oil changes. Unexpected repairs brought on by accidents or mechanical failures might also result in large expenses. Another significant aspect is fuel expenses, particularly for those who drive regularly or commute long distances.

The decision to forgo owning a car can be especially beneficial for digital nomads—people who work remotely and are constantly on the go. Reducing auto insurance, maintenance costs, gas, and payments can free up money. For digital nomads, this flexibility is crucial since it frees them from paying for a car regularly and lets them spend money on savings, travel, or housing. Furthermore, by not having to own a car, digital nomads can travel more freely, be it ride-sharing, public transportation, or short-term car rentals. For the price of a car, you can take many Uber journeys. This mobility fits with the digital nomad lifestyle, which emphasizes freedom, flexibility, and the capacity to work anywhere globally. It's not only a matter of convenience.

More money can be saved by diet simplification than you may imagine. Cooking at home is more economical and healthier. To cut down on waste, buy in bulk, stay away from packaged items, and use perishables sparingly. There are deli sections in many supermarket chains where you may get sandwiches and prepared items like mac & cheese or roasted chicken. These choices can lessen the strain and time associated with cooking. Think carefully before making a purchase. Consider whether you really need it or whether it's just something you want.

Additionally, purchasing quality rather than quantity will take you a long time. Take online courses or remote work into consideration as you adopt minimalism. Your travel and minimalist expertise can be a great asset. Additionally, search for low-cost or free entertainment options. Compared to pricey excursions, you'll be astonished at how gratifying these may be. And lastly, make wise travel decisions. Select off-peak times of the year to get the best airfare and hotel rates. Look into low-cost choices like Couchsurfing or hostels. Why not work while you're on the road? Possibilities such as teaching languages or participating in WWOOFing (World Wide Opportunities on Organic Farms) allow you to experience different cultures while earning money. By adopting minimalism, you can save money and develop a mindset of satisfaction with less. For a nomad, this mindset is extremely useful since it promotes adaptability, flexibility, and a more comprehensive, excess-free experience of the world.

Assign each room a purpose.

Every space should evoke a feeling. You may have some larger rooms with many uses, and you can divide one space from another. For example, you may define the den as the area where you and your family enjoy spending time together, watching movies or television, chatting, having fun, and engaging in recreational activities. Consequently, projecting a feeling of coziness and closeness there is appropriate. You may want to make sure the laundry room is set up so there aren't any piles. An atmosphere reminiscent of a spa can be created in the bathroom to create a lovely, opulent vibe. It is possible to have both comfort and a romantic vibe in the master bedroom.

Whichever room you are looking at, make sure your organization strategy is based on the purpose of each space and the overall "feel" you want the room to have! This will assist you in determining whether to relocate associated auxiliary goods from one room to another. If you plan to study or read, you will need a tall and modest lamp, side tables (for snacks), bookshelves, and a comfy chair or a recliner. It could be that the wall unit in your living room is overflowing with trinkets. If you intend to use that space frequently, it could be better to put your laptop on one of the shelves instead of trinkets. Why place it on your bedroom end table? Or keep it with you at all times. You don't have to use your laptop at the dinner table or in bed. Your apps and the Internet will live on without you! In this manner, you can converse with your loved ones in the dining room and sleep or have romantic moments with your partner in the bedroom.

Each room has one or more purposes. Anything that does not fit into those categories is probably clutter or lost. While doing this, make sure that your ideas consider livability and comfort.

Choose Your Starting Point

Most individuals are frequently tempted to start organizing and decluttering in the hallway, cabinets, and drawers under the sink. Although this is OK, starting with visible parts is more efficient and productive. Start with a simple task. First, choose the space that is the least messy and used. Because it requires letting go, decluttering can be painful. Starting with the room with the least amount of clutter can lessen the trauma associated with the process. It poses less of a threat. During the first practice, you participated in "Clutter Patrol," organizing and putting items back where they belonged. For example, you tidied up all the items on the tables, desktops, and countertops that weren't needed or were meant to be in this area and placed them in the appropriate rooms. But regrettably, you might have found that there was "leftover stuff" that couldn't fit anywhere. Larger items were also present, taking up valuable floor space. Those uncomfortable things will have to wait till later in your strategy. You can proceed to the cupboards, drawers, closets, counters, and shelves. Work your way clockwise around the room, starting at the door. We'll talk about decluttering techniques next. Make sure you focus on one room at a time at all times.

It is generally a good idea to begin in the room that is used the least, work your way up to the next room that is used less frequently, and so forth. The "Konmari" technique (Chapter 4) is slightly different. Whichever approach you select will rely on your cleaning preferences and personality.

In Chapter Two, the KonMari Method is explained.

In the previous chapter, we looked at Marie Kondo's biography, works, and inspiration for the KonMari method. Let's examine the KonMari approach in more detail in this chapter and see how it can be very helpful to you.

People have hoarded items they would never have thought to throw away and are throwing away clutter thanks to Marie Kondo and her method, which has become a global cultural phenomenon. Although the KonMari technique is a groundbreaking approach to decluttering, not everyone is a good fit for it. It's a strict and demanding process that could be too much for those new to organizing or who detest cleaning with unwavering zeal. These folks ought to begin cautiously before advancing to the KonMari technique. In any case, this answers the query, "What is the KonMari method?" An overview of the approach is provided below to assist you in determining whether or not to use it.

These sixteen items are just a fraction of what falls under the KonMari Method.

Item disposal: This method's primary goal is item disposal. Yes, even while the approach mentions tidying, it doesn't belong to make room for new ones. Since this strategy aims to get rid of items, hoarders are not the target audience.

According to Kondo, decluttering will be simpler if we eliminate more stuff.

Mentality

In addition to helping you physically declutter your home, Kondo's method will assist you in developing a more organized and decluttered attitude. She advises her clients to strive for an attitude that will allow them to consistently maintain their tidy state of mind rather than just cleaning and organizing their belongings once a month.

Large-scale Project

According to Kondo, you should declutter everything at once rather than taking things one step at a time. It will be challenging to revert to your previous behaviors once you have organized and disposed of items you no longer use. She thinks there should be a designated day or occasion for cleaning up.

It has nothing to do with storage.

Kondo has no say regarding shelves, racks, storage techniques, and other related matters. She thinks that "putting things away" gives the impression of organization, which makes it easier to ignore things.

Classifications

When organizing, according to Kondo, the key consideration should be category rather than location. This implies that you shouldn't clean a closet or a corner of your bedroom if you want to clean your room. Rather, choose a category such as clothing, books, etc. And organize anything that falls into the selected category. For example, if you are choosing clothes, get everything out of your room's wardrobes.

Everybody for one

The KonMari approach isn't very adaptable. It promotes using the same approach for every individual. As a result, it ignores "clutter" that has a particular place in some people's hearts.

Principles of Minimalism in Chapter One

A common misconception about minimalism is that it simply entails getting rid of whatever you don't need, won't use, or can't. Although minimalism does have certain aspects similar to that, it encompasses so much more. Before embarking on your minimalist path, it is essential to grasp the fundamentals.

Even if you feel uncomfortable doing something, it will be simpler to follow through if you know why you are doing it.

As you read, pay close attention to this definition of minimalism: it is a way of living that emphasizes the deliberate promotion of the things that matter most to us and, conversely, the elimination of everything that detracts from those things. This is a life that demands purpose. Therefore, minimalism compels us to improve nearly every area of our lives.

Eliminating the Superfluous

Most of us lead two or three separate lives, even if we are unaware of it. In addition to living one life around our neighbors, we live separate lives around our family, coworkers, and ourselves. Our true selves are most like who we are when we are by ourselves. We purchase items to help us look the way we want to because we don't want other people to notice it. We disregard our inner selves since our outward appearance is what we want other people to see. Because minimalism concentrates on the inner self, you can alter your outer self.

A minimalistic life is straightforward, devoid of extra items, and cohesive and coherent. Sadly, it is no longer instinctive to employ the concept of eliminating the unneeded. Rather, it's an acquired way of living that you may apply to any other circumstance. A minimalist lifestyle entails living the same life on Friday night, Sunday morning, and Tuesday night. It is steady, steady, and unwavering. It applies to all situations, all individuals, and all lifestyles.

Eliminating the extraneous, superfluous, and undesired is the essence of minimalism.

Easygoing

It makes no difference who we are daily: life can be utterly chaotic. To truly take care of ourselves, we are all too rushed, hurried, and worried. Even if we put in countless hours of labor for days or weeks to pay the bills, we never seem to have enough money at the end of the month. We run from job to school, to soccer practice, to the grocery shop, and back home again. Despite being a useful technology, cell phones have created us multitaskers who cannot concentrate on one task without trying to do another. What was the outcome? We never truly finish anything because we are constantly on the go, constantly thinking and acting. Ultimately, we believe that our lives are full, even though we are depriving ourselves of the solitude and happy connections in our lives.

By removing all that, minimalism sets us free from the current frenzy and enables us to concentrate and detach. It encourages us to limit our needs to those necessary for our happiness. It's important to understand that this doesn't mean having less only to claim you have less; rather, it means that if you really must buy anything, you should get one pair of shoes in a color that goes with everything, rather than five different colors that will take longer to match. To be simple is to remove the unnecessary and frivolous and retain the vital. You will recognize what is significant and crucial if you keep things simple.

Sticking to the essentials and simplifying things are hallmarks of minimalism.

Concentrate

Our society welcomes you into other people's worlds, promotes mass media consumption, and idolizes celebrities. The Kardashians' actions have greater significance to us than the actions of our children. We peruse periodicals, social media, celebrity gossip websites, and entertainment news to find out what's happening in the world right now. These individuals are promoted as the ideal by the contemporary media apparatus. Individuals who lead simple lifestyles don't care about who celebrities date or how they dress.

In contrast to how many others are, the media does not support them. They just don't mesh with the consumerist society that politicians and businesses support.

Rather, they focus on themselves and lead a simple, enchanting life.

Living a life full of peace, calm, and stability is the aim of minimalism. In contrast, most people are chasing after some version of a life full of success, glamour, and celebrity that they will never be able to accomplish. It challenges you to look at it and deliberate to slow down, consume less, and enjoy more. Many times, we realize we have been pursuing the wrong goals all along until we see someone who has a simpler life. You are ahead of the curve if you choose simplicity now and take the initiative.

Focusing on the actual and palpable while letting go of the unattainable is the essence of minimalism.

Cut off

To simply cut off contact with the outside world is the ultimate concept. Although minimalism has existed for decades, if not centuries, it has changed in a way that no other movement has in history due to the influence of contemporary technology. Disconnecting is one of the newest minimalist tenets. Learn to put your phone in a drawer or on your nightstand so that you may just be, rather than always having it within a foot's reach of your hand. Technology is fantastic and useful and can support you in your minimalist endeavors. But many of us lack the self-control to limit our phone use to when it's essential. We install apps, text nonstop, and never focus fully on anything we do.

Disconnecting from the digital world and concentrating on the actual one is what minimalism is all about.

Minimalism's Advantages

Put plainly, minimalism is a means of ending the excess that permeates our surroundings. That is the complete reverse of what every radio announcement and TV commercial promotes. Our culture revels in the amassing of material possessions; we devour the mess, fixation with material possessions, cacophony, indebtedness, and diversions that come with materialism. It appears that we are missing any true purpose. You can eliminate everything you don't need and concentrate on what you do need when you lead a minimalist lifestyle. The amount of stuff you need to survive and be happy could surprise you.

According to the hedonic adaptation idea, humans are innately capable of maintaining their levels of enjoyment. After a brief shift in perspective following significant happy or negative events, you quickly return to a normalized state of happiness. This has evolved into your genetic code to help you deal with the challenging conditions and unexpected events that life may throw at you. Instead of continuing to be a victim of your psychology, you may take charge of your happiness once you comprehend this idea and know how to apply it to your benefit. Examine this well-known consumer example:

When someone gets their Christmas bonus, they run out and buy a few flashy toys. At first, he is overjoyed and enjoys anything new since it makes him feel accomplished. But after a few weeks or months, they no longer fulfill him the same way and have lost some of their bright new feelings. The good news is that his tax return won't be delayed until May. He needs to buy more expensive stuff when May arrives to feel the same as when he bought the earlier items.

This ugly consumer-death cycle permeates every aspect of our culture. The depressing thing is that you are struggling with your mental health in addition to the marketing media's persistent indoctrination that you require more to be happy. However, you have another option. Examine materials with a minimalist perspective.

Minimalists resist acquiring more items because they know doing so will only provide momentary enjoyment. Furthermore, minimalists liberate themselves from needless clutter since they recognize that getting rid of their excess possessions would only result in a fleeting sense of loss or sadness. As a result, they spend less time buying and managing their belongings, freeing up more time to better themselves and the environment. Nobody can match the genuine, satisfying sense of accomplishment that comes from minimalism in terms of purchases.

Less is more.

Lowering your belongings is a necessary step towards incorporating a minimalist lifestyle. This integration has a few clear advantages: less cleaning time, less stress, more money, and increased organization. But before adopting the lifestyle, there are a few more perks that can change people's lives. Just consider the benefits of living with far fewer belongings.

Allowing space for what matters

Not only can you make space when you organize your drawers and closets, but you can also find serenity. You get rid of the constriction, which opens up your breathing. Make space in your house for meaningful things rather than possessions.

Greater liberty

Getting goods is like having an anchor; it always seems to bind you. A common fear among people is losing everything they own. However, if you let them go, you will feel a freedom unlike anything you have ever known: from debt, greed, needless obsession, and overworking yourself.

Putting hobbies and health first

You'll have more time to devote to the things you truly enjoy, the things you never seem to have time for, when you spend less time at the mall attempting, vainly, to keep up with the Kardashians in your life. Though most people claim to have too little time, relatively few ever take the time to reflect on how they are spending their days. You might be traveling, doing yoga, reading a book, going to the gym, or spending time with your children. Instead of doing what you love, which you should be doing, you're stuck shopping for more needless items at the mall.

putting less emphasis on material belongings

The things you surround yourself with are just filling a vacuum and serving as a diversion. Money can purchase a certain amount of comfort, but it cannot buy happiness. But your fixation with material goods and money should stop once you've satisfied this initial sense of comfort. Meanwhile, the media constantly bombards you with promises of happiness via more materialistic means. Recall that if having money and material goods was so advantageous, why do people not seem to have more than enough daily but still struggle? Why would you need more than one car since you will never drive all five simultaneously? Nor will you consistently wear twenty pairs of shoes at once. Avoid giving in to such cravings. There is no happiness on this empty journey. With frequent reminders that consumerism simply leads to a deceptive sense of enjoyment, avoiding falling into its trap is simple. While it's acceptable to enjoy things, you should equally acknowledge that you don't need them. Greater mental tranquility

You become stressed when you cling to material belongings because you constantly fear losing them. Your mind will become quiet once you simplify your life and separate yourself from these belongings. You'll discover that your peace of mind increases with the number of items off your plate.

Greater joy

When you simplify your life, the most significant aspects of it naturally draw you closer to happiness. The broken promises are readily visible through all the extra clutter. Additionally, since you are more productive, you will feel happy. Refocusing your priorities will help you become more focused, and when your life doesn't feel like it's always on the go, you'll be happier.

Chapter 2: Setting Priorities and Objectives

In this chapter, you will learn how to prioritize tasks in a way that aligns with a minimalist budget attitude. We'll look at how you might use a minimalist budget to accomplish particular objectives, like paying off debt or saving more money.

Decide what matters most.

You should be able to support your priorities with a minimalist budget. Therefore, it's necessary to reflect on and comprehend your objectives. It's acceptable for your objectives and driving forces to shift over time since your spending plan is also subject to change. Paying off debt, setting up funds for a particular purchase, saving for retirement at a particular age, or donating money to a charitable organization or your kids could be your top objectives.

Remember that every dollar you spend on other things takes you closer to your objective. It doesn't imply you shouldn't spend money; we all want to live our lives to the fullest and need necessities like food and shelter. But consider your aims and goals when making each purchase decision. Are the designer coffee and the discounted jumper more essential than your objectives? Several elements will determine your answer in each situation, but adopting a minimalist attitude will assist you in coming to the best conclusion.

If you're unsure how to define your objective, consider these suggestions. You can choose something straight from the list, something in combination with these things, or something tailored to your specific situation:

- Pay off debt: This includes debt from a car loan, credit card debt, education loans, medical costs, and obligations to friends and family. Managing debt can be quite stressful.
- Spend no more than your income: This objective can be combined with debt repayment. Even if you pay off all of your existing debt, you will always be in debt if your spending habits consistently outpace your income. If you haven't done this yet, this objective is a good first step towards achieving a better one.
- Save money in retirement accounts, emergency funds, and special expenses
- Consistently contribute a percentage of your earnings to a nonprofit or charity

you strongly believe in or have special meaning for you.

- Put money aside for a meaningful gift or occasion, whether for yourself or a loved one (such as a graduation, wedding, honeymoon, trip, or a significant purchase).

These are a few examples of the financial priorities you might find significant.

Taking Into Account When Determining Your Financial Priorities

When determining your financial priorities, you must consider your circumstances and what makes sense for you. Suppose your objective is something you are truly enthusiastic about, something you've wanted for a long time or something that truly speaks to you. In that case, you will more effectively adhere to your minimalist budget. Using your minimalist budget daily will help you feel good about yourself if you are progressing toward the financial objective that truly matters to you. You will truly feel content with every insignificant purchase you choose not to make since you are exchanging it for something far more meaningful to you.

Having a realistic outlook on the objectives or goals you establish for yourself is critical. A significant lifestyle adjustment may demotivate you if you are accustomed to granting yourself anything at your pleasure. Choose objectives you can sincerely commit to, then make an effort to live within your means to achieve these objectives.

The subject of ownership should be considered while determining your financial priorities. When obtaining items, focus on ownership rather than borrowing. Examine what vehicles or toys you can lease and what you can afford for payments to avoid going over your budget. Regarding the lifestyle you can afford, be realistic.

Think about the distinction between experiences and purchases as well. In reality, things don't truly make us happy on their own. Ultimately, experiences stick with us, even when made possible by purchases. Think about your objectives and the experiences that have significance for you. Can they occur without investing the same amount of money? For instance, are there any other activities that will strengthen your bonds as a family and yet be enjoyable and memorable without incurring the expenditure of a pool for "family time"? Does liking a certain sport require owning the newest, priciest gear to participate in it? Alternatively, is it possible to go and engage in this sport while spending less on the necessary gear? Analyze your priorities and decide where you may spend money and time on experiences rather than purchases.

Set a maximum of one or two goals to work on at a time while you define your priorities and goals. Monitoring multiple goals at once might become complicated. Another issue is managing your finances simply while accumulating money for various objectives. Choosing numerous objectives may result in a minimal savings contribution for each goal, and you might become disappointed as little progress will be made on any one goal. Keep in mind that living on a minimalist budget should simplify your life and make achieving your objectives simpler.

You should choose your objectives with that idea in mind.

Section Two: At Home

Have you ever wanted to arrive home in the evening to find everything in order and the home hospitable? Decluttering your home shouldn't mean eliminating everything you might need to create a cozy and welcoming atmosphere because being tidy doesn't necessarily translate into being welcoming. It entails getting rid of everything that detracts from your happiness. How many extra phones do you have hidden in drawers? What size TV do you require? How can furniture help you feel at ease instead of confining you? You must go through each room and eliminate anything that isn't essential to your pleasure. Give something to someone else if it doesn't make you happy. Offer it for sale. Clear stuff out and make some room in your house.

The mixes of colors, the various impulses vying for your attention, and the color schemes that entice you to hurry outside rather than stay warm and secure inside your house are the things that confuse the mind. At least four sizable boxes are needed for storing items. Remove the following items from each room as you proceed through it:

Items you haven't utilized in the previous six months

medications that have expired

Items you tried but found unappealing

furnishings that reduce the size of a room

Mismatched colors

Items that you dislike that you received from someone

Items of clothing you no longer wear

Things that are technological, electrical, and that you no longer utilize

Allow me to explain what has transpired for you. The deluge of information is holding you hostage. You've heard advertisements. Magazines have shaped you and made you a part of the consumer society you despise. Get rid of everything. Giving it out won't waste money. Arrange a garage sale and sell the goods for a profit. You may not be aware of this, but all the extra room you create in your house enhances productivity and makes life easier overall. Let me clarify how.

Your house gets easier to maintain when you thoroughly go through each room and remove everything extra as you clean it. By cleaning the room as you go, you may establish new guidelines stating that every room in the house should be left in a more organized state than when you found it, and you can ensure that everyone in the house is subject to the same rule. In essence, you are altering the atmosphere at home, and there is a tiny cost associated with that luxury if people wish to take advantage of its tranquility. It's not much to ask; giving kids a box to store their toys in will make their life easier. Your children are more likely to follow your rules if you make cleaning up easy for them.

Next, look at your living area and try to connect the indoor and outdoor areas. This could be as simple as adding lovely garden furniture to the patio or making your yard's plantings visible from your living space. This also helps because it adds to the tranquility of your home.

Work it out: You get more quality time with the people you care about if you spend more time unwinding and less time tidying up your house. More relaxation implies that you'll arrive at work each day feeling rejuvenated and ready to take on more. Happier people are more productive, and you will enjoy your home more if you can simplify and organize it to contain only the items you need rather than everything accumulated over the years. As mentioned at the outset. No, less will always obscure the artwork, so you are forced to observe it. The absence of clutter on the walls makes the colors stand out. You appreciate your kitchen more because your worktops aren't always cluttered with all the appliances you once bought but never got around to utilizing.

I adore how straightforward my house is, and it helps me think more clearly to organize my day without letting anything distract me. In addition, I was able to create a space in my house where

I could clear my head. This may be equally significant given that successful people frequently meditate or take pleasure in stress-relieving activities like relaxing and listening to music. People like Richard Branson, who will be the first to tell you that work and home life balance is essential and gives him energy, will be the first to discuss the topic. Your productivity declines, and everything is impacted if your home life is not fulfilling.

Types of Minimalism

Since no recognized categories or forms of minimalism exist, each person must determine what works best for them and how they wish to live. Certain variations of minimalism have gained greater traction than others. Living a mindful existence that you can more easily relate to is the aim of a minimalist lifestyle. I'm telling you to discover your own suitable, simple lifestyle because of this. For some, questioning and altering their behavior in certain circumstances is sufficient. Some wish to completely transform and turn their lives around. You will have to determine what is best for you and whether minimalism is a good idea.

The Essentialist

The name clarifies that this minimalist style focuses on the essentials. This can imply that you own the fewest, highest-quality possessions possible. A surplus of these items is only ballast; thus, the goal should be to have an enjoyable and long-lasting item rather than to save money. The guiding principle of this minimalist way of living is "quality before quantity." That does not imply that you should purchase more expensive but fewer items. Ultimately, it comes down to handling the products you consume more skillfully and thoroughly.

The Tight

The key for someone who identifies as minimalist is establishing and adhering to rigid rules. He wants to behave disciplined and, in a sense, prove something to himself. For example, you may set a default of turning to exactly 100 things. Ten of the 110 items are organized. Only the top 100 items are retained. We also allow a great deal of time for this minimalist kind to carefully consider what they wish to own. Strict regulations require that the intake of different items be carefully considered.

The Naturalist
Someone who leads a minimalist lifestyle distinctly defines, limits, and questions his range of action. As

previously said, minimalism frequently involves doing the environment a service. People need to adapt how they think based on the general manner in which they live. Because we are causing global warming if we do not lead minimalist lives. Humanity is continually at risk from the deadly internal effects of global warming. People act as though they might be easily replaced and as though they inherited the planet from their forefathers. But according to naturalists, it's the case that humans have taken over this planet from their progenitors. To implement this, naturalists are downgrading their ecological standing. For instance, they make use of Fairtrade or organic goods.

For example, people avoid driving because of the damaging effects of exhaust gases on the environment. For naturalists, the bicycle has become the primary mode of transportation. Naturalists also take matters like trash management and rubbish separation very seriously.

The Spiritual

This type learns to appreciate and know themselves better, focusing most of the attention and minimalism on himself. For this kind, self-observation and meditation are crucial. The mind is, after all, a plant of its vision that needs constant watering. We are always learning about ourselves on this never-ending path. We learn a lot of new things and get to know other people. As you are aware, learning never ends. The fact that so many individuals are drawn to this approach and desire to try it indicates that mindfulness exercise is becoming more popular overall. Because the inner core may be located and adjusted easily, trends like yoga activities are also becoming more popular.

First Chapter: Simplicity

Real minimalism differs greatly from what is shown in popular culture. Many people take their "minimalist" lifestyles too seriously, removing almost everything from their lives and living on almost nothing. This is frequently an illusionary portrayal of what minimalism is. Because of their shocking effect, these situations frequently draw attention and give the impression that leading a minimalist lifestyle entails suffering and deprivation. How happy can you be when you have nothing to meet your daily requirements?

You must first grasp what minimalism is and isn't if you want to be a true minimalist. Simply put, minimalism is the practice of living a life that only sometimes uses what you need. You make room in both your physical and psychic environments by removing or giving away everything that no longer benefits you or makes you happy. We shall investigate the idea of minimalism in more detail to comprehend this description more deeply.

True Minimalism: What Is It?

A life as a real minimalist would involve removing items that are no longer useful to you. Everything in your house serves a purpose and is regularly used, so there is no longer any clutter to be seen. Get rid of everything no longer useful in your life by selling, donating, or throwing it out. Your life is no longer spent gathering and preserving "treasures" in your house. Rather, you live a life devoid of materialism. Your life should be spent having no physical constraints, doing what you want when you want, and not worrying about accumulating more possessions. When you let go of your emotional ties to things, you discover serenity in life rather than in things that eventually become outdated.

What Advantages Do You Have?

Living a minimalist lifestyle has numerous significant advantages. First, clearing up extra clutter from your house has a mental healing effect. Observe five things you would consider clutter in the room right now. Give these items some serious thought and consider what they mean to you. Do they no longer make you happy? Or do you cling to them because they remind you of something from the past? Or do you just refuse to let go of things because you are too arrogant or lazy to let them go, so you just hang onto them and do nothing? Nothing good ever comes of the clutter we keep in our homes. We frequently feel bad about these things. We could have buyer's regret or guilt because we don't live in the same situation as before the item entered our home. We might feel angry with the object because it never goes away and continues to be a source of clutter and anxiety rather than just going away and ceasing to exist. We wish the thing would vanish because the weight of really having to get rid of it would force us to confront unpleasant feelings like remorse, hopelessness, and other unpleasant feelings. But when we get rid of these things, we also get rid of these feelings completely.

There are additional advantages to clearing clutter from our lives besides the psychological and emotional ones. For instance, preserving your possessions is easier when you own less of them. Clutter no longer exists, so you don't have to spend your entire life clearing it out. Everything you own has a place in your home that should be kept out of the way and serves a purpose. It greatly simplifies life.

Furthermore, you are no longer forced to labor furiously to preserve and acquire new possessions. You just need to produce enough money to get by daily; you don't have to pay to replace items that break or for repairs. You don't have to worry about leaving behind a house full of useless items that only serve to bind you down and make your life stressful and miserable. You may spend your free time doing whatever you like. You are free to relocate, travel, and engage in almost any activity you choose without being tied to your possessions.

Must You Let Go of Everything?

Remaining a minimalist does not entail throwing away everything you own. Rather, it indicates that everything that is no longer useful to you is being let go. Keep your painting supplies, for example, if you enjoy painting. However, if you don't enjoy painting, it's time to part with the supplies and keep them around "just in case you'll use them one day." You would have used them by now if you were planning to utilize them. Additionally, rather than buying all the supplies and then storing them away, you can buy fresh ones or even enroll in a painting class if you want to pick up a paintbrush.

Anything that actively contributes to your life is worthy of being retained. Anything that is merely retained out of duty or apprehension about running out when you need it must be thrown out. When we discover that we need new items in our lives, we may easily purchase them. Especially when we are not utilizing them, it makes little sense to carry around a wide assortment of useless goods. That's when your stuff turns into clutter, and clutter turns into stress, which makes life terrible. You must learn to part with what no longer serves you and hold onto what does if you want your life to change.

Will You Be Able to Shop Again?

You can, of course! Being minimalist doesn't imply that you will stop shopping or buying things. All it means is to be more careful about what you bring into your home. It is probably better to ignore an item entirely if you are buying something you know you won't use for more than a few days or weeks. In the worst situation, try renting one or lending it to a friend to determine if you truly enjoy the item. If not, just don't spend the money, time, or space on getting the item. Rather, go on!

Is There Any Joy in Any of This?

Putting in twice as much effort to get and preserve possessions is no longer necessary. Instead, by buying and storing less clutter, you may lessen the work you put into things. This allows you to perform almost whatever you want to do while also saving a significant amount of time. You have the choice to break free from the cycle of materialism and start truly enjoying life. You can begin living life to the fullest without being constrained by anything material. It will be simpler for you to pack up and move on as you won't feel pressured to spend as much time caring for and safeguarding your possessions. You don't have to worry about your material possessions limiting you from moving, traveling, or doing almost anything else. You won't have to work as hard to obtain what you have. Therefore you'll also have more spare time.

It's not entirely accurate to describe minimalism as it is presented in the media. It's not about having almost nothing in your life and existing in a severe condition of deprivation. If you're going to be a true minimalist, no law says you can only keep specific things or own a certain amount of objects. You can be a real minimalist and own anything at all. Ensuring that each of those goods is valued and that you will continue to utilize it is crucial. You can consider yourself a true minimalist as long as the purpose behind your possessions is right.

Recall that the goal of the journey is to bring freedom and joy. Getting rid of your possessions and making room in your home, office, and mind does not include putting yourself in an uncomfortable or novel circumstance. It's all about finding total relief from tension and discomfort and discovering how to live a more purposeful and happy life for yourself. It's about learning to live a life devoid of material possessions that don't even serve you and about combining freedom, pleasure, and joy in your life by breaking free from the cycle of consumerism. You will be able to take advantage of all the numerous values life offers when you learn how to live a really minimalistic life. You are prepared to begin day one of your 30-day minimalist challenge if you are ready to start living your life this way.

An overview of consumerism and minimalism

"Less is More." Del Sarto Andrea

Nothing is lacking in Minimalism. It's just the right quantity of stuff. —Graphic designer Nicholas Burroughs

The idea of Minimalism has grown in popularity over the past few decades and is now widely used both online and offline. What precisely is Minimalism? Why is it growing more and more relevant and popular? What are the benefits of Minimalism?

The necessities have more room when things are minimal.

There may be preconceived beliefs regarding Minimalism among some people. They interpret it as requiring restriction and sacrifice. Perhaps when people think of Minimalism, they associate it with spirituality, austerity, or Zen. Alternatively, they might choose minimalist fashion, architecture, and art. Some find Minimalism uninteresting and monotonous. Thus, they embrace maximalism in response. Conversely, some criticize Minimalism, claiming it's very strict and that individuals should aim for moderation and uncomplicated life instead.

All of these perspectives on Minimalism are extreme. While not wholly incorrect or irrational, they do not give a clear picture of Minimalism.

Fundamentally, Minimalism is an approach to thinking and living that promotes taking stock of one's existence and way of life, determining what is necessary, and getting rid of stuff to create room for one's genuine heart's desires. Minimalism is about living simply and in moderation. It's about striking a balance, and the heart is the pivot.

To help us understand this idea better, let's create some comparisons. If Minimalism and health are compared, Minimalism is about leading a balanced, healthful life rather than indulgent or yo-yo dieting. Using the financial industry as a metaphor, Minimalism is about spending money sensibly rather than being wasteful or frugal. Last but not least, regarding childrearing, it's about allowing your children the freedom to develop and prosper in the outside world, not about patronizing or neglecting them.

These examples demonstrate how simplicity requires balance. It concentrates on gains rather than losses, the good rather than the bad. It is freedom rather than confinement. Freedom from the vicious cycle of consumerism, debt, clutter, noise, diversions, and flimsy attachments. Freedom to prioritize relationships, well-being, contentment, wealth, and living out one's life's purpose and passion.

The analogies also demonstrate how Minimalism may be applied to all facets of life. A person may embark on a minimalist lifestyle with the primary intention of clearing out physical clutter. Still, they soon discover that the minimalist way of thinking permeates other areas of their lives, such as their family, finances, and health.

When you commit to simplicity, it appears to show itself in your life. It transforms you, and you start practicing its teachings every day.

In summary of the initial definition of Minimalism, Ignoring the myths surrounding it, Minimalism is about returning to the core of things and emphasizing what matters. It goes beyond merely making room for the sake of space. It's clearing room for what matters. Once you start this path, you discover that Minimalism is a continuous process rather than a one-time event; it is a tool to help you reach your life objectives rather than a destination. And you might discover that all facets of your life are positively impacted by it.

However, being minimalistic does not happen to everyone. You have to put it into action. You must put all into it. You have to go with Minimalism. This takes us to the second meaning of Minimalism—that it is a way of thinking and living.

Being minimalistic establishes a goal for you.

Advocate for purposeful living Laurie Buchanan stated: "Minimalism is about making space for a simple, meaningful life. It's all about living consciously.

Minimalism is indeed a matter of taste. It requires introspection on a personal level, which inspires action and intention that leads to a path that is individual to each person.

Minimalism has grown so popular that it is simple to forget about its distinctiveness. Typically, people only see the result.

Some people are fooled into believing Minimalism is just a maths game.

As an illustration, Introduce minimalist Carla, who lives in a Zen-like flat with just 100 possessions, but hey, Mike lives in a little house with about sixty possessions, so he beats her. Take a look at Sandra—she lives in a basic studio apartment and has only forty possessions! However, Rick outsmarts everyone because he only has 20 possessions, which he packs into his rucksack and travels the world with. But wait, monk Ling is the finest because he has nothing at all.

Colin Wright and other minimalist gurus are starting to debunk the myth that minimalist life is only about owning few possessions or being inexpensive by avoiding emphasizing how many things they own. You don't have to follow a particular lifestyle to practice

Minimalism since you have to figure out what works and what doesn't.

Another assumption is that men dressed in black clothing are typically minimalists. Perhaps a cliché like this might bring to mind pictures of well-known individuals who dressed the same way every day, like Barack Obama, Mark Zuckerberg, and Steve Jobs. When you read about them, you start to form preconceived notions about what a minimalist should look and behave like. However, there are various variations of Minimalism.

Minimalism encompasses much more than the outward effort (methods and practices like downsizing tangible belongings and streamlining wardrobe) and the external result (outcomes or manifestations like a clutter-free area and signature clothing style). Beginning with an internal process (awareness and choice), Minimalism eventually leads to behaviors and outcomes.

Without internal processing, external effort and results merely scratch the surface. While getting rid of stuff can help people restart their minimalist practices, people risk falling back into consumerist behaviors if they don't shift their hearts, minds, and values.

Conversely, the internal process may result in material austerity and spiritual asceticism, but it is limited to associate Minimalism with such outcomes. One can maintain a minimalist lifestyle even with ten children and a large home. A shoe collector who also practices Minimalism can derive delight from his hobby of amassing over a thousand pairs of shoes. One can pursue Minimalism while still pursuing his or her enthusiasm for trying out various cuisines. One can practice Minimalism and still wear an eye-catching, unique wardrobe. It is possible to practice Minimalism even if one decides not to start one's own business and stays employed.

Yes, the path to simplicity is distinct and personal. Something that you might not think is necessary in your life might be in another's. Its beauty lies in that. Let go of your opinion of what another person deems necessary, along with your non-essentials.

Another metaphor for this inside journey is to consider Minimalism as a self-awakening. We were introduced to consumerism as children thanks to marketing and advertising. Maybe we have been conditioned by our family, friends, school, work, and culture to embrace a consumerist mindset of conspicuous consumption, indulgence, or extravagance.

We might have become disconnected from our inner voice amongst all the noise until we eventually reach a breaking point where we become tired of the consumer cacophony and begin to hear a faint inner voice alerting us to the possibility that we might reevaluate our goals and priorities.

Chapter 2: Why Reduce?

Adopting a minimalist lifestyle affects your mental, emotional, and physical health. It has an impact on your finances, relationships, and job as well. Although there are both immediate and long-term advantages, it's important to remember that there will be drawbacks. Pros still exceed drawbacks in this case. You should think about Minimalism for the reasons listed below.

Locate Items Quicker

You'll be able to choose items more quickly if your closet is less crowded. Finding your work or hiking clothes will be simpler if you have 20 hanging garments rather than more than 50. On an average day, you might only be saving a few minutes. However, knowing if you're rushing to get to work or a client meeting is important.

Because tools and supplies are easily accessible, cooking takes less time. When your pantry, refrigerator, and cabinets are clear of clutter, it's simpler to determine what supplies you still have and what will expire before shopping for supplies.

In certain circumstances, you won't have trouble finding what you need if you merely store a few documents at home. These scenarios include going on a foreign trip, selling your home, submitting a loan application, and filing taxes. Furthermore, retrieving those few documents rather than boxes of papers will be easier if your house is destroyed by fire or flood.

This tool can search for computer files in a matter of seconds. That function might not be helpful if you have thousands of files and most of the details are lost. Organizing fewer files makes it easier. Additionally, creating backups for them is faster.

It is most useful to find items more quickly in an emergency. If your car key is the only item in your drawer, pocket, or tabletop, you can get it immediately. You can also bring paperwork and other necessary stuff if there aren't many.

Reduce the Time You Invest in Cleaning

Having fewer possessions implies cleaning less of them. But this won't occur right away. Clutter must be removed first. This could require more than one day.

Big vases, heavy chairs and numerous tables are always harder to hoover clean. Even washing surfaces is easier when there are no lamps, vases, magazines, or other centerpieces to move. You will have fewer dry leaves and twigs to pick up if you don't have many indoor plants.

Making your bed with just one or two pillows only takes a few simple steps. You'll wind up with a bunch of throw pillows you have to kick and throw off your bed to obtain some sleeping space if you try to recreate those pictures of perfect beds. Then you have to pick them up and rearrange them when you wake up. Another task on washing day is the pillowcases for those scatter pillows.

If no decorations are hanging on your walls, you can refinish them faster. Removing and rehanging those mirrors, paintings, certificates, and pictures is exhausting. If you have wall decals, you must also clean the remaining adhesives. If you've been a minimalist for a while, there won't be many things on the floors, counters, and tables to pick up. Therefore, you don't need to spend hours making your house appear nice if you're hosting guests.

Steer clear of unnecessary spending.

Being a minimalist allows you to cut down on a lot of expenses. Finding things more easily will save you money on replacements. Furthermore, you won't be as apt to neglect occasionally checking the status of your belongings if you own less of them. You can identify possible issues at their earliest stages by conducting routine inspections. As a result, those issues will be resolved, and more significant damages that call for costly repairs will be avoided.

If you only bring a carry-on bag for your trip, you won't have to worry about paying more for checked bags. You can keep your valuables safe when you're gone from home. If you have a few valuables that you want to keep safe, you don't need a large (and more expensive) safe.

Even if a shopping bag could be inexpensive, purchasing three or more bags each time you go shopping will undoubtedly add up. Conversely, reusing implies that you just have to make one investment. Eliminating numerous personal care products that perform the same functions as their generic equivalents might save you money. (Consider body mists, colognes, perfumes, and scented body lotions and soaps.)

You won't require expensive cleaning services if your home isn't overly cluttered. Also, you are limited to using the standard dumpster. It's not necessary to pay for pickup and rent a large one.

If everything you own fits into one vehicle, your moving expenses will also be reduced. Requirements for packing materials will decrease. You might just need to hire a truck and enlist the assistance of close friends to help you pack, move, and organize your belongings if you don't have many breakable items. You can choose the smaller moving companies if you still want to work with one. They won't feel as stressed by managing little belongings even if they only have a small number of employees. You have less money to tip when there aren't many employees.

The answer? Less is more.

I did not intend to close Chapter 2 on a sad note, but it is precisely the picture that will give you a genuine understanding of how modern, developed-world reality is structured.

There is a route out, which is wonderful news. You are not required to continue on the never-ending treadmill of more. It's a pointless treadmill. You will simply run in circles, requiring increasing things to make you happy. The worst thing is that you're stuck in this race to the bottom. The idea of simplicity offers an escape route.

All that remains of minimalism is the adage "less is more." That should seem somewhat familiar to you. This is an old Zen Buddhist proverb. The concept of "less is more" means letting go of perceived or external demands to concentrate on what is actually important.

You get back control of yourself when you let go of things. As I said before, I'm not talking about living in abject poverty, shaving your head, signing a poverty vow, dressing in sackcloth, and spending your days in a monastery on a mountain, chanting from sunrise to sunset. I'm not in favor of that. That is not in the slightest monastic.

Even though you have fewer possessions, you're still out in the world, interacting with others and savoring each day as it comes. You reclaim something so precious by letting go of things—most notably, your mental addiction to them and what you believe they mean to you. You take control of yourself again. Put another way, you reverse all kinds of mental conditioning for yourself by letting go of things that you truly have no control over.

Why should I care so much about myself? The only person you can manage on this earth is yourself, as you most likely already know. Yes, you are the only one over whom you have complete control. To put it plainly, you get yourself, power, and a true identity when you let go of the games the world plays.

Reduce your reliance on outside factors and honor your own beliefs.

When you practice minimalism, you will engage in a significant amount of communication. You trade in external items for something else, mostly your addiction to them and your perception of their significance. You receive the chance to discover inner truths in exchange.

Realizing that you are not trading truths for goods is crucial. No one—not even me—can say that. Rather, you are basing your happiness on external things because you are preoccupied with existing things. You were unaware of these inner facts or blind.

These facts haven't changed over time. They remain true long into the future, were true yesterday, and are unquestionably political and pertinent today. They are here to stay. Your willingness to examine them is what shifts. Your receptivity to even observing them at all shifts as well.

This is the point at which things start to shift because you start focusing on the outside world and believe that you are someone merely because you own certain items. This is because you're falling for the group hypnosis or group lie, which is the belief held by others that those who possess particular items are significant.

I've already explained Where something originates and what it's a part of in Chapter 2. You're releasing yourself from that. You are discovering inner truths again and celebrating them. As an illustration, consider the truths of compassion, pride, self-love, respect, and love.

You have to give others what they want before you can get what you want. The irony is that when we let go of external objects and our need for them, we uncover the layers that have distorted our perception of who we are. Our universe no longer revolves around us.

More, more, more and me, me, me are no longer the main priorities. Rather, you give yourself the authority and the green light to prioritize others over yourself. Simply put, prioritize relationships over possessions. Genuine comprehension and deference preceding rank, authority, and structure.

All of this initiates a domino effect. These are not merely pleasant emotional epiphanies, nor are they intellectual concepts that elevate you above others, as if you could look down on them and declare, "I'm superior to all of them because I'm transcendent and philosophical." I'm this system-opposing rebel. That isn't how it is. Rather, it starts with humility, reorients your sense of self-worth, and redefines your needs.

It starts at zero because once you realize how these inner truths operate, the importance of selflessness becomes clear. Try loving someone else if you want to experience love.

Did you know that the only person who can completely and profoundly feel love is the one who is offering love? Did you know that forgiveness is required when there has been a prior misunderstanding and that knowing something is much better and clearer as a result?

The huge falsehood that arises from the truths I shared in Chapter 2 is that the more you consume, the more of a tractor beam you become. To put it another way, this entails moving away from the tractor beam of the self. It is untrue. You truly become smaller and smaller, more sensitive, and feel entitled to a variety of things until, at some point, all you're left with is a delicate, hypersensitive person who is unable to handle stress. You're going to break otherwise.

What Is Minimalism, Chapter 1?

The definition of minimalism is not predetermined or standardized. Like simple living, minimalism can have varying interpretations among individuals. You must know exactly what minimalism means to you if you want to learn more about it.

What is the minimalist movement?

"Minimalism is simply the perfect amount of something, not a lack of something," argues renowned minimalist Nicholas Burroughs.

There is more to minimalism than just material possessions. Focusing on and making a commitment to the basics rather than squandering time, effort, or money on details is what minimalism is all about. "Minimalism is the deliberate promotion of the things we value most and eliminating the rest that distracts us from it," noted minimalist Joshua Becker said to us.

For most of us, minimalism is clarified and simplified in the definition above. Being minimalistic means knowing exactly what matters most to you in life.

Focus on the things that occupy most of your thoughts, time, energy, and space, and then consciously clear out anything that stands in the way of your treasured possessions. Diverse individuals possess varying interpretations of minimalism. Each of us has particular values that are particular to us.

The secret to minimalism is attention.

What in your life are the most valuable and significant things? Although you own many items, you will see that only a select handful truly add value to your life when you concentrate on the most significant and worthwhile aspects. Minimalism is recognizing what you don't need in your life, much like where not to invest. After that, take it off and continue to feel at ease.

Being minimal is a method.

Achieving minimalism is not the goal. It's about pushing yourself forward consistently. Leaving only the things that are essential to you. A daily evaluation of your priorities is part of minimalism.

Time is important in minimalism.

When you concentrate on what matters most, complexity disappears from your life. You are now free of false beliefs, anxieties, guilt, and worries. You offer yourself more room to breathe when you limit your possessions to what is necessary. You spend more time with less as you become more adaptable. Focusing on your most valuable resource, time is made possible by minimalism.

What isn't minimalistic

Numerous myths exist regarding minimalism. Here are a few of them:

The goal of minimalism is to rid yourself of everything. You don't have to give up everything to be minimalist. What you stand to gain by removing items that don't enrich your life should be your first concern.

Living simply is more difficult: Minimalism does not make your life more difficult. On the contrary, living a minimalist lifestyle makes things easier for you.

Minimalism and frugal living are synonymous: Saving money is only one aspect of minimalism; the other is not the same.

Likewise, the idea that minimalism is solely appropriate for young, single people is untrue.

Minimalism solely pertains to your possessions: While removing unnecessary items is crucial, minimalism is more than just focusing on your possessions.

What Are Your Desires?

Why did you come here? Take a moment to consider that. Do you wish to cut costs? Would you like more spare time? Would you like to worry about less clutter in your life? Do you wish to lead a simpler, more contented life? What are your desires? It's okay if you're still not exactly sure what you want.

I'm going to assume that if you're considering adopting a minimalist lifestyle, you're primarily interested in financial savings, stress relief, and increased flexibility. These three factors mostly influence my lifestyle choices, while there are many more reasons to lead a minimalistic one. Even though your motivations may be different from mine, don't we all ultimately desire to live lives with greater freedom and contentment?

Simple living does not entail making a vow of poverty. Billionaire Warren Buffet has spent decades living in the same small home. He is aware of the situation. Money is not the main focus of modern minimalism; rather, time and freedom are. Warren Buffet has wealth but wouldn't be as free if he invested in a huge estate. In addition to paying extra taxes, he would also need to hire groundskeepers and cleaning staff and find something to put in all those vacant palatial rooms. Not everyone places a high value on mansions. What matters to you? Whatever your financial situation, you may reduce costs and lead a more independent, simpler life. So buckle up and join me as we delve into contemporary minimalism.

Dark Holes

I would like to start by discussing black holes. Everybody has dark spots in their lives. You will find it easier to adjust to a minimalist lifestyle the fewer of them you own. Black holes will impede and undermine your efforts to live a minimalist lifestyle. They'll squander your valuable time, deteriorate your health, and break the bank. I've lived a modest existence but have had many dark moments. With time, they have evolved. Over time, they will come and go; you will always have one or two. The goal is to minimize their presence in your life.

You will be drawn in by Black Holes and have your life sucked out. Steer clear of them at all costs. If you cannot avoid them, try limiting your consumption. A black hole delivers little to nothing in return and consumes your time, energy, money, health, or other resources. Your shift to a minimalist lifestyle will be smoother the sooner you eliminate black holes in your life.

On TV

A 2016 Nielsen Media Research research found that the average American adult watches television for five hours and four minutes daily. Over 77 days a year are covered by five hours and four minutes daily. More than twenty-five months of TV per year. In other words, the average adult in America will watch television for one day out of every five. Every five days. What percentage of that time will the typical adult American spend reading? What percentage of that time will they spend in the great outdoors? What percentage of that time will they give back to the less fortunate? What percentage of that time will they use to make art or music?

I start with television since it's one of the most pervasive and sneaky black holes. Though it's the silent killer, it's not always one of the most hazardous black holes. It's the one who draws you in and, without your knowledge, devours your life. It looks like something very innocent. Why can't I watch Breaking Bad, House, or X-Files episodes in one sitting?

Since just before I relocated to the West Coast, I had not owned a television. I might do so eventually, but I haven't given in yet. The only way to take stock of an experience and determine its impact on you is to remove it from your life. I've realized how pernicious television is in my years without it. I have no moral objection to television. I don't want to start a protest at Best Buy or go on a crusade against it. I just want people to acknowledge how dependent they are on that box. I want them to consider what true value their television provides. I posed a challenging question to myself before I gave up watching television: Your age is eighty-five. Your loved ones are gathered around you as you lie on a hospital bed. You're reflecting on the significant achievements, insights, and errors you've made. How likely will you think, "My God, I wish I had watched more television"?

Never.

I would never want that, and I'm ready to wager that I won't be thinking about television until I'm 85 years old—whether or not I've started watching it again by then. I now ask myself this question all the time. "When I'm 85 and dying, will I look back and wish I'd done more or less of this thing?" I ask myself while deciding if anything is truly worth my time. I usually leave if the response is that I think I'll regret having done less of it. I will keep doing more of it if I believe that after I look back, I will regret not doing more.

When I look back, I wish I had taken more trips. When I look back, I'll regret not writing more. I'll regret not juggling for longer. I'll regret not having found love sooner. I'll regret not doing more for my fellow humans and animals. Looking back, I regret not making a bigger difference in the world. I will regret not being more fearful and more forgiving. I refuse to reflect on my life and regret not watching more TV.

www.ingramcontent.com/pod-product-compliance
Lightning Source LLC
Chambersburg PA
CBHW052144110526
44591CB00012B/1845